10 MURDERING REASONS 95 PERCENT OF ONLINE ENTREPRENEURS ARE BROKE

How To Join The Top 5 Percent Cashing Out Consistently

Kingsley Okoro

The Kings Organization

CONTENTS

INTRODUCTION
ARE YOU STRUGGLING TO MAKE MONEY ONLINE?

Naturally, the internet is supposed to have made the life of an entrepreneur pretty easy. At least, you no longer have to wait until you have certain amount of money to rent an office or store before launching out as an entrepreneur.

In fact, you don't even need to have your own products to be in business these days; thanks to the Affiliate Marketing and Network Marketing industries.

Marketing and making sales has also become a lot easier today than it used to be for businesses in the past, thanks to the internet.

An entrepreneur today can literally launch his own business and sell to customers in different cities, or even countries, just with his smartphone or personal computer.

What this means is that, as an entrepreneur in the 21st Century, the internet has put the world in your palm.

There's no limit to what you can achieve with your business.

But, if it is really true that doing business today have become much easier than it used to be in the past, why do we have many online entrepreneurs who are struggling?

Why do we have more than 95 percent of online business owners who are broke? Why are many quitting their online business to go back to getting a job?

These are the questions I will be answering in this book. I hope that after reading this book, you'll be better equipped to avoid all the pitfalls that hold many other entrepreneurs down and you'll begin to see possibilities of becoming very successful in your online business.

But what really is an online business and why do many people get scared at the mention of the name "internet business"?

Simply put; any business transaction that can be conducted via the internet is an online business. If you have a way of putting out information about your business via the internet, and completing a business transaction without needing to have a physical location, you are in the online business or internet business.

As you can see, there is really no special industry set aside to be known as "online business".

Nearly every kind of business can operate online today. Some can operate 100 percent online; while others may need to combine both online and offline operations to work.

3 Kinds of Businesses

There are basically 3 kinds of businesses you can do on the internet today:

1. **You can start a traditional business** where you own the company, the products and the brand. You could also start a retail

business buying other people's products and retailing them for profit, or if you have a skill, you could set up a service-based business, using your skill to serve people's need and getting paid for it.

With the help of the internet, you can literally do this business without having a physical shop or office.

2. **You can become an Affiliate Marketer** promoting other people's products and earning commission on every sale.

The difference between affiliate marketing and a retail business is that in affiliate marketing, you don't get to buy and stock any product. You also don't have to handle product delivery, or customer service. You are simply not a helpdesk. All you do is recommend other people's products using your unique affiliate links.

When someone buys the product direct from the owners of the products, you get your commission. You literally do not have to be there when the transaction is done or when the product is delivered.

3. **You can join a Network Marketing** company and become an independent distributor making money from selling their products and also building your own network of distributors.

One powerful thing about a network marketing business is that your income does not depend on your effort alone.

Unlike in affiliate marketing where you don't get paid unless someone buys any of the products you recommend via your affiliate links, the network marketing business allows you to build a large network of other independent distributors and make money from every sale they make.

The keyword here is "network". This is the singular word that makes the rich richer.

What Online Business is Not

In an attempt to make money online, many people have become victims of scammers who disguise as online businesses, designing pyramid and Ponzi schemes they used to defraud people of their money. This is the main reason most people have a wrong impression of the term "online business".

Today, a lot of people believe that anything that has to do with the internet is a scam. That's a wrong mindset born out of ignorance.

I believe the problem most people have is they have no proper understanding of how business work. So the moment they hear promises from get-rich-quick scheme peddlers, they get carried away by greed and laziness, and they buy into any such promises that they can actually get rich without putting in any work.

This is why people lose money online and tag the internet to a bad name.

The problem is not the internet; the problem is people thinking they can get rich by simply giving their hard earned money to someone they barely know, who promised to invest for them and pay them huge returns.

If all you do is give your money to people with hope of earning back huge returns, you are not an internet entrepreneur; you are simply a gambler betting your hard earned money on fake promises of get-rich-quick.

You simply patronized money "doublers" who sold you what you wanted to hear.

Who This Book Is For

This book is written for true entrepreneurs, not gamblers. It is written for people who try to leverage the internet to do honest, reasonable business of providing value in form of products or services.

It is written to help real entrepreneurs avoid common mistakes that are killing their chances of scaling their businesses and making the level of income they desire to make.

Each chapter represents one reason that is keeping 95 percent of entrepreneurs broke and tips on how to avoid the pitfalls. If you follow the lessons in this book, you will never have to struggle to make money with your business.

In fact, building your online business will become fun rather than a struggle.

Whether you are using the internet to sell your own brand and products, or you are building a multi-level marketing business, or you're simply promoting other people's products; the information in this book will help move you away from the 95 percent of online entrepreneurs who are struggling to make money, to the top 5 percent who are crushing it in their businesses.

So if you're one of the true entrepreneurs I am talking about, then, follow me while I walk you through on how to make your online business journey extremely profitable.

REASON 1:

YOU THOUGHT IT ALL WRONG

I had already dealt with this in my introduction, but I still had to make it the number one reason most online business owners are broke.

We all know how powerful our mind is. In fact, when it comes to business, your mindset is the one who decides whether you will succeed or fail. The battle is won or lost in your mind, even before it becomes reality.

Not An Escape From hard Work

A lot of people think doing business online means you've found a shortcut to riches. And that's why many quit the moment they realize the amount of work required to make their business successful is really no different from the amount of work needed to succeed offline.

Whether you're doing business online or offline, you must understand that business is business.

A business owner must concern himself with issues of generating leads and making sales. The only different is
that an online entrepreneur knows how to generate leads and make sales leveraging internet tools; while an offline entrepreneur focuses on marketing and selling his business physically (offline).

But whether you are an online entrepreneur or an offline

entrepreneur, one thing is common among all entrepreneurs: they all want to make sales consistently.

"Sales" is what brings money to the business. Selling is what makes sure the business remains a business. If an entrepreneur cannot find a way to drive in sales consistently, he risks losing his business.

And this is the part many people who want to make money online miss. A lot of people think that by choosing to do an "online business", they get to avoid the work involved in selling. That is why they fall victims of scammers posing as investment platforms.

Why Scammers Are Thriving

Investment scammers understand that majority of people want to get rich but do not want the hard work associated with having to sell.

They know a lot of people want the reward without the work; so they capitalize on this wrong desire to design a system that will promise people exactly what they want to hear.

This is how Ponzi schemes and pyramid schemes came to become a thing. This is why, no matter how many times people lose their money, many more people will still continue to lose.

I've had people come to me asking me to recommend an online business that can make them money. But the moment I give them my recommendations, they run the other way simply because it often involves "selling" of products or services.

In fact, I've had a friend say to me, "Kings, I really need to make money online. I need to have another income apart from my job. Can you show me any opportunity that won't require me marketing or selling anything?"

When I asked to understand what he really wanted, he went on to explain, "I just need something I can just put in my money and allow my money work for me. I don't have time to marketing or look for customers who would buy something or downliners to join my business. I just want to invest my money and be receiving my returns".

Well, I simply had to explain to him why I couldn't help him.

I don't believe there is any legit means of making money that does not involve providing some form of value. I told him that if he wanted to be an investor, he should try the stock market, or simply move into real estates.

But he still needed to be careful not to fall into the hands of scammers, because they're practically everywhere.

In my opinion, investing is a skill one has to learn before investing his money into any asset. Simply handing your money to someone you hope can invest for you is the biggest risk I see people take...a risk that has caused them more loses and pains than gain.

So, if you've decided to be an entrepreneur, then be an entrepreneur. Don't go into business with the mindset of a gambler hoping for "one big hit." Sit down and build a real business that will grow into a consistent income stream.

What Are Your Expectations?

One reason most online entrepreneurs fail is because they quit too soon. One reason they quit too soon is because they come into business with the wrong expectations...and this cuts across any kind of business or industry.

Because many people have no proper understanding of what it means to be an entrepreneur, a lot of startups will quit as soon as they don't start seeing the kind of income they expected early enough.

Most people assume that simply posting a few product images online will drive the sales in; so the moment they don't see that happening, they give up.

I have come across a lot of network marketers and affiliate marketers who quit their businesses simply because they weren't making the big money they were promised before they got involved.

Many people join these businesses with wrong expectations due to the promises made to them by the people who sold them the opportunity.

You must understand that a lot of these affiliate marketers or networkers are simply interested in getting you to sign up so they can get their commission. They are practically not interested in helping you succeed in the business.

This is why I always tell people to take control of their business as soon as they start. Don't bank your future on the attitude or behavior of your upline. This is your business; it is your responsibility to figure out a way to make it work.

Your upliners or leaders are there to offer mentorship and guidance, but if it happened that you got the wrong leaders who aren't interested in mentoring you, you must take control of your business and begin to seek out knowledge and skills you need to succeed in the business.

As an entrepreneur, having expectations of success is critical; but you must have the right expectations. Never believe in getting rich quick. Never expect to make millions in the first few months of getting started.

The Job Of An Entrepreneur

You must also know that in business, challenges are to be expected. The job of an entrepreneur is to solve problems. You can't quit on your dreams simply because you encountered challenges.

People with the wrong mindset expect things to be easy. So the moment they run into challenges or difficulties, they give up. A lot of online business entrepreneurs I've met stopped marketing their business simply because people weren't buying.

So, instead of learning how to make their marketing work, they simply give up with the mindset that it doesn't work and will never work. But hardly will you find any successful entrepreneur who did not go through the phase where nothing was moving.

If you quit simply because things got difficult, then you were not really ready to achieve your dream. It means your dream was never really important to you in the first place.

Successful entrepreneurs consistently seek knowledge and solutions; they don't just quit because things got difficult. If you wish to succeed in your online business; this is the kind of mindset you must develop...the mindset of a winner.

Rather than give up when things are not working, you should ask yourself, "what am I missing? What do I need to learn in order to make this work?"

Having the right mindset will help you stay on your business long enough to make it work. There is no such thing as get rich quick. The only shortcut to wealth is to learn from someone who has more experience in what you're hoping to do.

So instead of thinking of quitting when things are not working out in your business, think of learning new skills, new strategies, and new approaches. After all, there are many ways kill a rat.

REASON 2:
YOU LACK PROPER BUSINESS SKILLS

Everyone knows that to become a successful doctor, one has to undergo proper training in a medical school. To be good at fixing computers, you must have first acquired the skill of a computer engineer.

If you needed an eye surgery, there's no way you will allow someone without the skill and experience of a surgeon to touch your eye, no matter how motivated the person sounded.

We all understand how important skills are in making one successful in every other profession, but for some reason I still don't know, majority of people do not think that success in business requires having good business skills too.

So, a person wakes up in the morning, fully pumped up with motivation to quit his job and become his own boss. And the next day, he gets busy investing his life savings into a new business, hoping that motivation alone will make him successful.

Few months down the line, his business hasn't picked up yet, and he gets discouraged. He isn't making enough sales, which means he isn't making profits. Cost of running his business is eating up his capital and the only reasonable option left is to quit and go back to looking for a job.

"Maybe this business thing is not for me", he concludes. "Maybe it is true that some people are born to be entrepreneurs and others are not".

Well, I don't know about people being ordained entrepreneurs at birth, but what I do know is that each time I meet someone like that; it usually doesn't take 20 minutes to figure out what their problem is. And most times, they all have the same problem.

Doing Business Without Becoming Entrepreneurs

Many people want to become successful in business, but have never read a single business book from cover to cover. Nor have they ever taken a course on marketing, or sales, or negotiation, or copywriting, or digital marketing.

A lot of entrepreneurs think that paying for an online course, or training to learn skills, is a waste of money. Why should they, when they already are naturally gifted in the art of selling? Why pay for courses, or coaching programs, when they can easily Google out whatever information they need?

Most of these people understand that you can't perform a surgery in a hospital without first undergoing training to become a surgeon. They also understand that you can't fix cars unless you have first become an auto engineer through years of training.

But when it comes to business, they don't seem to recognize the place of training and knowledge and skills. They want to do business without first becoming entrepreneurs.

The Only Shortcut To Success

You see, I will repeat what I mentioned in the first chapter: The only shortcut to success is learning from experiences of people who have walked the path you're hoping to go.

Business is an art. Selling is an art. Management is an art. Leadership is an art. Relationship building is an art. Communication is an art. And because they are all arts, you must learn the skills if you must succeed in them.

You can't claim to need success when you are not willing to pay the price for success. And often times, the only price you get to pay for success is acquiring knowledge and skills and then working hard implementing them.

10 Skills For Building An Online Business

I'll just come clean with you, and you must take this very seriously. If you want to succeed with your online business, there are skills you must acquire…skills you cannot afford to joke with. It doesn't matter how much you have to pay to learn these skills; see it as an investment rather than an expense.

1. Copywriting – This is the most important skill every entrepreneur must have. This is the number one skill that will ensure you never go broke again.

Copywriting is simply the ability to sell with words, or to use words to compel people to take the exact action you want them to take.

It is possible to always hire a professional copywriter to write your sales copies whenever you need them, but as a startup, this could be too expensive for you. And I also believe that sales copies, if they must really communicate the mind of the entrepreneur, should come from the entrepreneur himself.

But regardless of whether you are learning the skill yourself, or you are hiring a pro copywriter, just know that no online business could ever succeed without the skill of copywriting.

2. Lead Generation – Having the best product won't do you any good if people don't know about it. You need to learn how to get into the crowded internet and social media, and selectively attract the right kind of audience who would find your product relevant, and then use your copywriting skill to sell the product to them.

Many online business owners want to make sales but have no way of generating leads consistently. There is a reason big companies continuously invest millions into adverts; it is because without a consistent flow of leads, the business will run out of sales.

Internet marketing is more than just posting images of your products on Facebook and Instagram. Learning how to generate leads through targeted ads on Facebook, Instagram, Google or YouTube; and then converting them into customers, is a priceless skill any entrepreneur should acquire.

3. Presentation – You must learn to pass your message in form of a presentation. Creating presentation videos that share your message and sells your products is a great way to leverage the online space for business growth.

It is often said that the greatest business leaders are also great speakers. No wonder many business leaders invest so much money acquiring public speaking skills. They understand the power of words in communicating their vision.

I found that leveraging marketing tools like a presentation video generates lots of sales for my business without needing me to do the presentation every other day. All I need to do is create one presentation video where I talk about a particular product and this video can go on to sell to thousands of customers in the future. It is a great way to enjoy leverage.

4. Email Marketing – Growing your email list should be top priority. It is the only real asset you own as an entrepreneur. Email marketing skill is not an option; it is a must for any entrepreneur.

Social media platforms, like Facebook or Instagram, does not belong to you. The owners can decide to log you out of their platform for no reason. I recently had a YouTube Channel I created shut down by Google and everything I tried to get it back failed.

So, if everything you do in business begins and ends on social media, you are playing a dangerous game. You could lose everything in an instant.

This is why email marketing is critically important. Anyone building an online business should get serious growing their email list. Your email list is your own asset. Nobody is going to take that away from you. Nobody is going to decide what kind of messages you send to your subscribers.

I once heard Brain Tracy say that even if he lost all his wealth today, he'd get it all back in a few years because of the high quality email list he has built over the years. He's right!

5. Content Creation – We live in social media age. Content creation is a skill that will help you build a solid brand that people will come to know, like and trust to do business with.

Whether it is creating video content for your YouTube channel, Tiktok or Instagram; or written content for Facebook, Twitter or LinkedIn; or whether it is growing a blog on your website; people need to hear your message and get value from you consistently.

Content creation skill is critical, if you must become an authority in your industry.

6. WhatsApp Marketing – Many business owners still think WhatsApp is for leisure, when this is, in fact, becoming one of the most powerful tools for growing a business today.

You need to invest in learning the tricks and strategies for leveraging WhatsApp for business growth. Stop wasting the most powerful tool the internet has handed you.

7. Funnel Building – If you are already making a lot of money, you could hire someone to handle your website and sales funnel building, or simply outsource it each time you need it.

But if you're just starting and don't have the budget yet, it is important you learn how to use sales funnels for growing your business.

My life changed when I learned how to build sales funnels for my business.

8. Creating Offers – Many entrepreneurs think it is their products that people pay for. No! What people pay for is the offer you create around your product. An entrepreneur's job is to consistently create new offers that will drive cash flow into the business.

An offer is the reason why a customer should buy your own products instead of one of your competitors'. Offer Creation skill is an invaluable skill to have as a business owner.

If you combine the skill of creating irresistible offers with a good copywriting skill, your pipeline will never run dry and you'll never lack money ever again.

9. Follow Up – Just because someone read your powerful sales copy and saw your great offer is not a guarantee they'd buy immediately.

In fact, if you show your offer to 100 leads, at a success rate of 10 percent, only 10 people could buy immediately. And these are the 10 people who were already in the buying mode. They were already in the market for your product.

They probably didn't buy because of how great your copy was. They bought because they were already in desperate need of your product. But only a few people will ever be in this buying mode. So what happens to the remaining 90 who didn't buy immediately?

This is where follow up comes in. Most of the people who see your offer may still not buy immediately, and that does not mean they don't like what you're offering.

It could be they're not ready to buy yet, or they're still skeptical. You know a lot of these people have been disappointed by online merchants in the past.

People want to take time to be sure they can trust you. Some of them might be having doubt that you or your product would be any different from the ones they've tried in the past.

So if you just let them go after the first exposure, you're going to be losing a lot of sales, because most of them could still buy after more exposures from you.

Statistically speaking, most customers will only buy after you've contacted them the seventh time. So as an entrepreneur, learning how to follow up properly is a skill you should go for.

10. Sales Closing – This is usually where most people miss it. It doesn't end with generating traffic and making them offers; you must learn how to ask for the money.

Sales closing skill will help you know how to strategically ask for the sale, even when the customer is still having doubt.

Many of your customers will never be able to make up their minds to buy until you help them make that decision. Sales closing is you helping them to make the buying decision.

There are many digital skills one could learn, but most of them can be outsourced to third-party experts. But the skills I mentioned above are skills you must invest your time and resources into learning and perfecting. They are skills that will ensure you never go broke ever again.

REASON 3:
DO YOU REALLY UNDERSTAND
WHAT YOU ARE SELLING?

This may sound funny, but a lot of online business people really do not understand what they're asking people to buy, and this is mostly common with affiliate marketers and network marketers—people who are promoting products they didn't create themselves.

It is true you don't need to create products of your own before you can become a business owner, but that does not excuse you for not having proper understanding of what you are really expecting people to buy from you.

Most entrepreneurs easily get carried away with the claim that the product sells itself. No matter how popular you think the product is or how much you feel people need it, you must know your products from a user's point of view.

You must be able to explain how this product can solve your customers' problems and why you believe it is their best option. You must be able to defend your product and explain why your customer should choose it against other competitions.

Learn Everything You Can About What You Do

Even if you are not the creator of the product, you must take out time to research and understand your industry.

You must understand what kind of problems your product is meant to solve. You must understand how that problem affects people and what exactly they need from you.

It's Not About You

Being in business is not all about how you feel about your products; it is about how your product will affect the lives of people. You must understand that it isn't about you; it is about them (the people you are hoping to help).

This is why just providing superficial information about your product may not be enough to make people buy. They get such information everyday online.

At the end of the day, people will only buy from those they feel have better understanding of their needs and has demonstrated how their products can help them solve that need.

If you are creating content around your niche; you must realize that people won't get sold if all they get from your content is still pretty much the same information they get from everywhere else. You have to go the extra mile to provide more vital information that addresses the area of their needs that nobody else is talking about.

I have heard network marketing leaders telling their downliners to simply copy their own content and repost on their social media handles.

While that may seem helpful, you must know that simply reposting or regurgitating someone else's content will not make you stand out. And when you don't stand out, there's really nothing that will attract people to you.

So take time to do an extensive user experience research about your industry and products. And if you can, use the products yourself to get firsthand experience of how it really works. Using the products yourself will provide you the big picture of what kind of help your product can provide for people, and this will put you ahead of someone who is just copying and pasting other people's content.

Become An Authority In Your Field

If you are in network marketing or affiliate marketing business, or even a traditional business and you realize your leaders or competitors are selling more than you, it could be because people tend to believe them better.

The reason people believe them more is because they know everything about their products and they know how to communicate their message to their audience, to make their audience perceive them as an authority in the field.

Until people begin to see you as an authority in your field, there's a limit to how much you can grow. Your competitors will eat you alive if you keep playing at the surface level.

When it comes to business, your KNOWLEDGE, your SKILLS, and the power of your MESSAGE; are your unfair advantage. These will keep you relevant and make you stand out in your industry.

Learn everything you can about what you do. And continue to put your message out there. Get known. Always show up in their faces. Increase your online presence.

Speak boldly about what you do and how you can help people. Be the one person people think of whenever they have a problem related to your niche.

REASON 4:
ARE YOU LOST IN THE CROWD?

As a business owner, understand that the product you are marketing is not the real asset. Your company is not the asset. Your compensation plan is not the asset. You are the asset!

You are the person people want to buy from. You are the person people will follow; not the company or the product.

No matter the industry your business falls under, you must know that you are not the only person operating in that industry or niche. There are lots of people competing for the same customers you're fighting to get and keep. And most of your competitors are richer; more experienced and have better resources and personnel in their business.

It gets even worse if you are in a network marketing business. Because, not only are you dealing with other networkers in other companies who's product line is similar to yours; you are also dealing with thousands of other distributors in your own company, who are all marketing the exact same products you're selling.

This is why many online entrepreneurs are not growing. They're simply lost in the crowd. No one knows of their existence, because people have lots of options to choose from.

How To Avoid Getting Lost

So how do you avoid getting lost in the crowd? It's simple: STAND

OUT!

People get lost in the crowd because they're trying to blend in. To fit in. To be like everyone else. You can't stand out if you're busy trying to be like everyone else. And you won't get noticed by your customers if nothing stands you out.

The internet is crowded. Every day, customers are faced with lots of options to choose from, and most of them are confused. They don't know who to trust to deliver the solution they're looking for.

Most of the people you're hoping will see your post and buy from you are skeptical. They've been disappointed countless times by online business people and they have become more careful. Most of them won't just send you money because you post beautiful photos of your products—they see similar posts from other people online.

How To Make People Trust You

To win their trust and loyalty, you need to change strategy. You must turn on your creative powers and find your uniqueness. Your message must be different from what the crowd is chanting. Your packaging must be different. Your delivery system must be different.

One mistake a lot of small business owners make, in their attempt to beat the competition, is to keep cutting down prices. By doing that, many have gone bankrupt. In their attempt to make more sales, they ended up killing their business.

Cutting prices in order to beat competition is not always the best approach. Customers will be happy to eat you alive if you keep doing that. Remember that customers don't care about the survival of your business; they only care about themselves.

One way to stand out and beat your competition is to communicate the value of your product rather than just talking about your product. When everyone else is talking about product, stick to talking about the value they get from buying from you, from working with you, from doing business with you.

It could be free shipping, or additional service you provide to help them get the best out of your product.

Regardless of price, people are more likely to buy from someone they feel is out to help them solve their problems, as opposed to someone who is just out to sell.

If you are in a service business, you must make sure your customers believe in you so much they'd be willing to pay you twice as much as others are asking for, for the same service.

And this can only be possible when you have taken time to communicate the value of working with you to your customers.

If you are in a network marketing business, instead of just talking about how great your company and compensation plan is—which is what everyone else in network marketing is talking about—you could do something different.

You could focus on communicating the value of working with you —of being a part of your team. You could focus on letting people know what they stand to gain by following you, by working with you or by being in your team.

Let people know how much value you bring to the table and how working with you guarantees they grow faster, they make more money and they struggle less.

Remember that a lot of people have tried and failed in network marketing in the past. Most of them already know that a big part of their failure can be attributed to poor mentorship and support from upliners.

So when you concentrate your message on this area, these people will easily relate to your message and will come to believe you better than those just screaming "join my company!"

That is how to communicate value when others are simply talking features. That is how to stand out from the crowd.

What Customers Are Looking For

I have had a lot of customers buy from me even after complaining that my product is more expensive than others.

So, I have come to realize that, at the end of the day, what customers are truly looking for is the best value. They want the highest quality product or service, with a great customer experience, at the best possibly price.

Being able to answer the most troubling questions in your customers' heads, even before asking them to buy, is one way to communicate your true value. This is where content creation plays a huge role.

People need to perceive you as an authority in your field;

otherwise, you'll just be like everyone else asking them to buy.

So it goes without saying, that a serious business owner must invest time into learning and improving on his ability to stand out and be unique, and to communicate this uniqueness consistently.

Your uniqueness is what makes you a magnet that attracts the right customers to your business, when others are busy hunting and begging for customers' attention.

REASON 5:
STOP GOING ONLINE TO SELL

Here's what I'm actually saying: Many online business owners are not successfully driving in sales simply because they go online to sell.

Now, before you tell me how crazy that sounds, let me explain.

As a business owner, you do need to make sales. That's why you are in business after all. But just as you are looking to make sales, other businesses are looking to make sales too.

The customers you are hoping to sell to are already bombarded with sales pitch from different businesses every day. Many of them are tired of coming online to hear or read another sales pitch. They want something different.

They don't want to easily believe another sales pitch because the last time they did, it didn't end well. The person probably didn't deliver on their promise, so they ended up disappointed. So right now, they don't easily get attracted to content that says "buy me".

But these people do have problems. Many of their problems are ones your products can provide solution to. But how do you get them to even listen to you, or pay attention to what you are selling?

Stop Selling And Start Giving Value

Generally, most online entrepreneurs would just go online to market and try to talk people into buying what they're selling; but most often, that doesn't work.

This is why going online with the motive of selling isn't going to get you sales. You should go online to do something different: Give Value.

Giving value simply means you go online to post helpful information around your niche that can educate, inform and sometimes, entertain your audience. It means sharing information that can help someone solve a problem, without asking them to buy anything.

There's one thing you must know about selling online. It is that people will only buy from you if they feel like they know you, if they have begun to like you, and most importantly, if they feel like they can trust you.

Remember that people are skeptical. Most people won't just buy from you because of your wonderful sales copy.

They need to feel like this isn't just another hustler with a good sales pitch trying to get their money like the last one they encountered.

What this means is that selling online requires patience. You need patience to build trust in the hearts of people. You need patience to consistently provide value for free, so you end up becoming a favorite in the hearts of your audience.

As an entrepreneur, building quality relationships with your audience is the best marketing strategy you can employ. Your customers must begin to see you as someone who truly care about them rather than someone who just wants to sell them something.

Always Take The Attention Home

Apart from creating helpful content on social media and having lots of loyal followers, smart entrepreneurs and digital marketers know the importance of taking the attention home with them. This is where email marketing is needed.

Bringing people to your email list and feeding them with helpful tips and information daily or weekly will help make this relationship more personal. Because right now, you can send targeted emails that sounds more personal than when you're just posting on social media.

So that's the point. Don't be like everyone else. Don't go on social media to sell, go there to build relationships by adding value and making people know you, like you and trust you.

And when the time is right, you can then show them how your product or service can help them solve the problems they have.

REASON 6:
YOUR CONTENT HAS NO FOCUS

What do people know you for?

That's one question a lot of people don't ever ask themselves. I have seen many online business owners whose social media activities have completely no connection with the business they're into.

They simply go online and post whatever they feel like posting for the day, whenever they feel like posting. Many business owners only remember to post content on social media when they have a new beautiful picture to show their friends, or during their birthdays.

If you are serious about building a successful online presence, you have to get intentional with your social media activities. You are not just coming online to catch up with friends anymore; those days are gone.

You are now a serious business owner. Whatever you do online right now is either adding to the growth of your business or it is detracting from it. Your activities are
either helping to build your brand or they're destroying your brand. There's no in-between.

This is why you need to sit back and plan your social media life right now. You need to draw a plan of what you must do online and what you must stop doing.

- Which of the social media platforms should you focus on?
- How often should you post?
- What kind of content should you post?
- What kind of content should you not post?
- When should you talk about your product?
- How can you connect with your social media friends on a personal level?

You need to answer these questions and use it to draw a plan of your social media activities to make it relevant to your goal of building a solid brand and growing your business.

Focus On Your Niche

Understanding your business and knowing the niche to focus your content on will help prevent confusing your audience. People need to know you for something.

While you are allowed to be versatile, there has to be one particular area people see you as an authority in. There must be one area that comes to the mind of people as soon as your name is mentioned. This is what we call a niche.

The mistake many people make is they are busy posting content online with no focus on a particular niche. So people like and comment on your posts, yet they cannot really say which area you are an authority in.

Such behavior will hurt your brand and kill your chances of building a successful online business.

Eric Worre became a world-class name by focusing on a particular niche for many years and building a solid brand as a Network Marketing Coach. Robert Kiyosaki has remained at the top of his industry by maintaining his identity as one of the greatest Personal Finance Educators of all time.

If you must succeed online, you must choose a niche and focus on it for a very long time. And make sure your niche is in line with your line of products.

Stop Confusing Your Audience

Don't post content about relationship today and tomorrow you're talking about politics. The next day you're talking about music. And another day you are an expert in health. You're simply confusing both yourself and your audience.

If you are building a business in the fashion industry, you must make sure more than 80 percent of your social media content is fashion focused.

You can share content that educates people with tips on how to make the best of their fashion budget. You can share content of how to dress classy on a budget. You can share content on how to make your cloths last longer and remain new.

Content creation is all about using valuable information to engrave your name in the hearts of people as it relates to your line of business.

One day, when they're in need of someone to solve a problem that has to do with your business, who's name do you think would pop up in their minds first? Yours, of course!

And that is because you've been the name and face behind all the relevant information they've been receiving regarding that niche.

And if they need someone they can trust to deliver, who is a better option than someone they already know as an authority in the field?

REASON 7:
HUSTLER OR BUILDER?

There are two kinds of people I've come to meet in the online business space:

1. The Hustlers, and
2. The Builders.

Hustlers are people who are just concerned about making money today, regardless of how it comes. They just want to get the next sale, get the next commission, or cash out today.

Builders take time to strategize, plan, and then execute with a goal of building something that would last. They are not merely interested in getting paid today; they're interested in getting paid for life.

Hustlers don't necessarily have the patience to build something strong before they start making money. If they can't get the cash coming today and tomorrow, they often quit and jump into the next opportunity that promises quick money.

Most often, the people who fall victim to fraud are people with the hustler's mentality. Because they have no time to research and learn about the opportunity before investing into it, they often bank their success on mere promises sold them by other hustlers looking for desperate people to defraud.

The Worst People To Have On Your Team

If you are in a business that requires sponsoring people or building a team, like the network marketing business, hustlers are the worst kind of people to have on your business team.

They hardly have any ideas to contribute to help the business grow, and they hardly have time to learn, get trained, or work hard.

Hustlers would join your business if you promise they'd make a lot of money; but what they hardly pay attention to is the part of the presentation that talks about the work that needs to be done.

Regardless of the line of business you get into, you cannot go far with the hustler's mindset. You need to drop that mindset and pick up the builder's mindset. You need to remind yourself daily that you're in this for the long-term.

Builders Plan Before They Work

One day, while teaching his audience, Jesus asked; "Is there any of you who would want to build a house and would not first sit down to plan himself and to count the cost of completing the project?"

The first thing about builders is they do not work without a plan. Before they even set out to start building their business, they must sit down and draw a clearly defined goal with a plan they must follow.

If you are really serious about building a successful business online, you must first plan yourself. You can't afford to approach your business with the "whatever the day brings" mindset. You must be in control of you daily actions as it relates to your business.

Builders know that not everyone is their customer. So they take time to study their market to know what kind of people they should focus their marketing message on.

Builders also understand that there is a difference between hunting for customers daily and attracting customers to your business. So they focus on building systems that will consistently attract the right audience to their business; while leaving the hunting for the hustlers

Plan To Be Better

Builders understand the value of learning continuously. So they always set aside a budget for their personal development and skill acquisition.

They understand that the most important part of planning to become successful is planning to become better every day. Hustlers, on the other hand, think registering for training is a waste of time and money.

I once had a young man who registered into an online program I belong to. It's an online business school that trains people on digital marketing skills...including the skills I talked about in chapter 2.

Because this business school uses the affiliate marketing system to promote their programs, and their commission payout is quite huge, most people misunderstand it to be some sort of pyramid scheme.

I think the confusion comes because one has to be a registered member of the business school, before he can be allowed to partake in the affiliate program. And this is exactly what happened to this young man I'm talking about.

This young man had to quit the program barely two weeks after he joined. He got angry that none of his friends were buying into the program via his affiliate link; so he concluded he couldn't succeed in it.

When I tried to reach out and to advise him to take out time to watch the digital marketing training videos he got when he registered, he simply said he didn't have time to watch any training. He said he thought he'd just start making money just by joining the program.

Here is a young man with literally everything he needed to become very successful at his disposal. The quality of digital marketing courses he had access to just for being a part of this program; training courses that would've literally turned him into an expert digital marketer, and would've made him very rich in the long run, yet he cast it away like a piece of rag.

This is the same program that has completely transformed the lives of over 10,000 African youths, and have empowered them with capacity to make money whenever they want.

Yet, all this young man cared about was that he shared his affiliate link with his friends and they refused to sign up to the program so he could earn commission.

That explains why hustlers struggle. They ignore the most important investment of all: an investment in themselves.

Like I have said earlier in this book; to be successful, you must be willing to pay the price. And when it comes to building a successful online business, the only price you have to pay is learning and working hard.

In fact, when you consider that learning would empower you to work from a place of enlightenment; then it wouldn't be hard work anymore, but "smart work".

Once you develop the habit of learning, and then back it up with hard work with a long-term goal; there is no reason you won't become rich in the long run.

Hustlers Hunt For Customers; Builders Attract Customers

Having a builder's mindset will empower you with capacity to build a proper digital marketing system that drives sales on autopilot, when other hustlers are busy jumping from inbox to inbox, spamming people with sales pitches and wondering why no one is buying.

Having a builder's mindset will enable you stay on the cause, even when the money hasn't yet started coming in. As long as you are busy building your system, it doesn't really matter how long it takes to complete, you are rest assured that once your system is up and running, your income stream will begin to throw in consistent cash flow, even when you are sleeping.

And that's what builders do; they build with the big picture in view. Because they know that they don't have to keep working hard for money for the rest of their lives.

REASON 8:
RUNNING AFTER THE NEXT SHINY OBJECT

There's a young man I used to know from years back when I newly got involved in the network marketing business. He was a typical example of what the bible would refer to as "unstable", or "easily brown apart by wind of doctrine".

This young man never stayed with one network marketing company for more than a year. He was always moving from one company to another. Always coming to me to promote his new business that he was sure was far better than every other company he'd tried in the past.

The problem was, the next time I would meet him, he would've dumped the so called best company and was now promoting a different one. Needless to say, he wasted all those years and never really recorded any form of success in any of those businesses.

This kind of people are not only found in the network marketing business; they're in every industry. I remember a young lady who started posting her new fashion business online.

She was selling readymade male cloths and shoes. Few months later, she realized the fashion business was not going well, and she moved into selling bedspreads.

It didn't take long and she stopped selling bedspread and began posting cosmetic products from a network marketing company. The last time I spoke with her, she was tired of the cosmetic business. She said people weren't buying.

In fact, she said she was tired of anything business. That she believed business wasn't for her. She was going to dust her CV and look for a job.

It's Not About The Business; It's About The Entrepreneur

The truth is nobody could ever succeed in business without focus. You must be able to tune out all distractions and focus on making your business work.

There is no good or bad business or product. There are only good and bad entrepreneurs. If your business isn't producing result, it doesn't mean the business is a bad business, or that your product is not needed.

The setback you're experiencing is simply an indication that you still have a lot to learn. The truth is, many people in that same business, selling the exact same product, are making millions from their businesses.

That proves that the problem is not the business. The problem is the entrepreneur driving the business. Your business is like an airplane and you are the pilot. You are the one responsible for whichever way your plane flies.

So, stop jumping from one shiny opportunity to the next shiny opportunity. That attitude is what hustlers, or gamblers, are known for. They never stay at a place for too long, especially when they aren't making the quick money they hope to be making.

Builders don't easily get distracted, and that's because they're working with a plan. One advantage of having a plan is that it keeps you focused. You don't easily get distracted by external objects and forces.

Is Social Media Helping Your Business Or Killing Your Business?

Another form of distraction many online business people struggle with is distractions from social media. Nearly everyone doing business online is prone to this form of distraction. Personally, it took me a long time to learn how to overcome this distraction.

Most people spend hours checking their Facebook, Instagram, email, etc.; while doing little to nothing that produces result in their business. You must learn to focus your attention only on productive activities.

While social media can be useful for growing your brand presence and attracting more leads to your business, unchecked use of social media can be detrimental to your business growth. Social media can be a huge distraction taking you away from activities that should produce good result in business.

Not all social media activities are productive. Just because you are busy online doesn't mean you are productive. Channel your attention to activities that brings in more sales and money, and limit the time you spend on every other activity.

Success Requires Productive Hard Work

I have studied the lives of many super successful people and I know they are very focused and hardworking. They hardly waste time on frivolities. They hardly waste time on activities that don't bring money to the business.

There are activities that may be necessary in your business, but are not critical. An example is checking emails every minute, replying comments on social media posts, etc.

Spend less time on such activities, or delegate them to someone else, while you focus on money-moving activities like writing sales copies, creating offers, setting up new marketing campaigns, creating new promos, creating content, etc.

The money-moving activities are your top priorities as the business owner; everything else is a distraction until the critical activities are completed for the day.

REASON 9:
HOW IS YOUR COMMITMENT LEVEL?

There is no substitute for hard work; but I guess we all know this already. People often recognize the importance of hard work until they start their own online business.

Most employees would commit to a culture of waking up early in the morning and preparing for work every single day. And when they get to work, they put in all their energy to their job without feeling like they're doing anything out of ordinary.

The need for hard work and commitment seems more real to people when they have a boss who could fire them. But as soon as they launch out to become their own boss—especially as online entrepreneurs—they often seem to forget the importance of hard work and commitment.

It's still a wonder to me how people react when they realize that the online business they just started requires some level of hard work. Most people often think that because it is called an online business, then it should mean getting rich without doing any work.

I think majority of the people are simply misguided. I mean, why would you agree to put in so much hard work and commitment to working in someone else's business, but when it comes to running your own business, you won't even commit 10 percent of that hard work to make your business work?

What Is Motivating You? What Is Driving You?

We seem to have a generation of people who are simply motivated by fear—fear of getting fired. Fear of losing their job.

That explains why a person who wakes up at 5am every morning and goes to work all day, will not even commit 2 hours every day to building his own business.

Here's another funny part: Most people, when searching for job, can afford to write and submit countless applications and attempt many interviews, and will never give up until they finally get a job. But when these same people eventually start an online business, they will not even have the balls to prospect 10 people before giving up.

I once met a young lady who spent two years after graduating from university writing and submitting over 50 job applications and attending over 40 interviews, yet she kept getting turned down.

One day, an older friend advised her to stop searching for job and start a network marketing business, which she eventually agreed to do.

Unfortunately, this young lady only lasted 2 weeks in her network marketing business before quitting and returning to the job hunt. Her excuse? People weren't buying. Nobody was accepting her opportunity.

When I inquired how many people in total she had spoken to about her new business, she told me she spoke to about 7 of her friends and neighbors. And when they all turned her down, she decided that the business wasn't working. So she quit.

Now, this may sound ridiculous, but I have actually met so many people with this same attitude. They can be persistent and committed until they start their own business...especially a form of home business.

Why People Easily Quit In Online Business

I believe the number one reason people behave like this towards a home business or an online business is because this is the kind of business that doesn't require huge capital investment to start. So people easily give up when things aren't working out fast enough, simply because the investment is money they can afford to lose.

Try starting a traditional business with an investment capital of N5 million, most of which is probably borrowed, and tell me you'd quit the business and go back to looking for job just because you tried for 6 months and your business didn't kick off.

I believe that people involved in a traditional business are more likely to persist and to put in a high amount of hard work into growing their business simply because a traditional business often isn't easy to start. So much money and energy must have gone into getting that business off the ground.

But the truth it, whether you are starting a traditional business or an online business—whether your startup capital is N5 million or N20,000—your business will never become successful if you do not put in a high amount of hard work and commitment to it.

I could say you should simply go back to becoming an employee, if you're not ready to work hard, but the truth is, you still have to work very hard, if you must avoid getting fired from your job. But instead of working very hard making someone else rich and living each day with the fear of losing your job, why not put in that same hard work into building your own business and making yourself rich?

The Hard Truth

There's no sugarcoating it; the truth is your business will fail if you do not put in hard work and commitment to it. And I don't care what sweet talk was used to brainwash you into believing you could have it any other way.

If you're looking for a get-rich-quick scheme to invest in, you shouldn't start a business; not even an online business. What you should be doing is gambling or giving money to professional money-doublers and praying they don't disappear with your hard earned money.

I guess the point I'm trying to make is that success requires hard work. And that includes success in an online business.

I've met a lot of idiots who sign up into an online business of some sort and quit the next month because the money they were told they could make suddenly wasn't falling from the sky. I call them idiots because I believe only an idiot would expect to get rich suddenly just because they bought a membership. Starting is only starting. To grow the business and see money coming, you must do the work—every day.

You must wake up every day with pure determination to commit to your business and to see it grow. This is about your dream —your dream of gaining financial freedom. If your dream is important to you, then it must reflect in the way you run your business.

Financial Freedom Has A Price

Freedom is achievable, but it won't come without a price. If it was that easy, everyone who has ever attempted to do business online would've become very rich.

The only reason the online business is full of stories of failures is because most people are coming into it with wrong expectations. People think starting a business online could be a shortcut to wealth.

If you have read to this point, you already know there is no substitute for hard work. Success is a reward for hard work in business. So don't be like those idiots going about spreading sad stories of how the online business doesn't work, when in reality, it is they who wouldn't put in the work.

My Biggest Fear

Every one of us is motivated by some sort of fear. While employees are motivated by the fear of losing their jobs, I choose to be motivated by a different kind of fear: the fear of not fulfilling my dream of financial freedom.

Rather than working hard all my life to make other people rich, I choose to wake up each day inspired to work hard building my own business. After all, the best thing a job can offer is temporary sense of financial security; not financial freedom.

I call it temporary because you're never in control. You could wake up one morning to meet a sack letter for no justifiable reason. But building your own business will afford you freedom for life.

My biggest fear is living all my life without enjoying true financial freedom. Just the thought of struggling financially all my life is enough to scare me into working as hard as is required to make my business grow and my income scale.

True, entrepreneurship is not easy; but the reward at the end of the day is worth the price you pay in the process.

So what do you choose to be motivated by: the fear of losing your job, or the fear of spending the rest of your life never having a taste of true financial freedom?

Only you can answer that!

REASON 10:
HOW PERSISTENT IS YOUR PERSISTENCE?

There a famous story I love to tell each time I speak on patience or persistence. You probably may have heard the story, but I'll go ahead and share it here because it helps drive the message home.

It's a story of a man who owned acres of land where he was digging for diamonds. After digging for quite a while without finding diamonds, he gave up on the quest, sold his land and went on to another city in search of greener pasture.

What then happened next was amazing. The man who purchased his land decided to continue with the mission set out by the original owner of the land, which is digging for diamonds. But he approached it quite differently.

Before continuing the digging, he decided to bring in some experts who knew how to figure out where diamonds are located and where they aren't. These experts came in, examined the land, and told this new owner that, not only does this land have acres of diamonds buried under it, but that the diamonds are actually just a few feet under.

What that means is that the original owner had already done most of the digging and was just a few feet to the diamonds he was searching for before he gave up. All this new owner had to do was dig a few more feet and he would become stupendously rich.

Quitting Too Soon

Many people are like the original owner of that land. They start something and quit just because the results they hoped for isn't showing up quickly enough. And most times, they give up just when they're almost about to hit their breakthrough.

I think the online business is where people tend to give up too easily. I believe it is mainly because most people come online to look for quick fix. They want quick money to solve their imminent money problems. And when they are not seeing fast result, they quit.

There's an advice I usually give my students, especially when they're just starting out in the online space: Regardless of how big or how little your startup capital is, see your online business as a million dollar investment.

I then go ahead to ask; "Would you quit on a business you invested a million dollars to start, just because you worked at it for 6 months and it isn't as profitable as you hoped?"

The answer I often get is "no". Most people would persist in the business until they make it work, if they knew a million dollars was at stake.

So the key is to see your business as a million dollar business, even if all you invested in starting was N10k or N20k. Work hard on it as you would a business that cost you one million dollars to start.

A Hobby Or A Business?

If you don't treat your online business as a serious business—if you don't work at your business as though your life depends on it —that business will never grow as big as it needs to be.

If you treat your online business as a hobby, it will pay you as a hobby. If you take your job more seriously than your own business, be rest assured that your business will never grow to set you free from the employment trap.

There is another way to look at that advice: Treat your business as though it was already paying you a million dollars monthly, even if you haven't started making any money yet.

It is the power of becoming. We all have that power. The power to project our thoughts and actions into the future we want. To live as though our dreams had already become reality.

There are times I would caution myself to not speak in a certain way, or behave in a certain manner, or mix up with a certain kind of people. The reason I would give myself was that rich people don't speak or act that way, or rich people don't roll with such people.

I started living that way, even when I was struggling to find my next meal. I always reminded myself that my reality was not where I was; my reality was the future I desired the most. So I would task myself to live in the reality I desired.

That same attitude has helped me to stay persistent in business, even when it wasn't showing any good signs of success. I would always think and act as though my business was already a multimillion dollar business.

If anyone tried to talk down on my business or to convince me to quit and do something else, I would be very angry, because they were advising me to quit a million dollar business to go get a job.

To be able to push through the hard times—the times when things are difficult—you must find an excuse to keep your mind focused on the task. You must never give in to thoughts of doubt and failure.

The original owner of that land gave up acres of diamond and traveled to a faraway city to search for greener pastures. He had wealth and power lying under his nose all along, yet he missed it simply because he could not hang on just a little longer.

Other People's Knowledge, Other People's Expertise

There is another reason the original owner of that land lost that opportunity of a lifetime; and this is also why most people who try to do business online fail:

That man had no way of knowing that he was standing on top of acres of diamonds, simply because he did not seek the services of experts who knew more about diamonds than he did. The second man was able to change his life fast enough because he did what the first man never did: He secured the counsel of experts.

I see a lot of struggling entrepreneurs who have never paid for a training or course before to learn how to make things work. They simply try to figure things out on their own, using their own limited knowledge, and when things don't work, they quit and believe it isn't for them.

The truth is, the only shortcut to riches is investing time and resources to learn from someone who knows better than you. No amount of money spent acquiring knowledge is ever wasted.

The ability to leverage on Other People's Knowledge and Expertise is what separates the small players from the big players.

Companies will spend millions each year bringing the best minds in business to their board of directors or advisors because they understand the value those people's knowledge and expertise can bring to their overall financial statement.

Most small business owners think they are saving money by doing everything on their own.

I never knew how easy it was to become successful in online business, until I started paying money to coaches who trained me with high value skills required to succeed online...especially the skills I mentioned in chapter 2.

My life and business changed when I began to stack up my skillset with high income digital skills, like website and funnel building, copywriting, social media advertising, graphic designing, presentation, video editing, email marketing, etc.

With these digital skills, it has become easier today to sell anything online, than it ever was when I didn't have those skills.

Surround Yourself With People Who Help You Succeed

Another shortcut that is helping me is surrounding myself with coaches and experts—people I could easily run to when I get stuck —who have a wealth of knowledge and experience that could prove invaluable when needed.

Many people struggle because they try to do it all alone. And it's not their fault. Working alone is all they have known their entire lives.

From being punished in school for trying to collaborate during test times, to having to compete against their colleagues at work so they can get a promotion; many people have never experienced the power in teamwork.

There is a reason professional athletes make a lot of money and armatures don't; that's because professionals have coaches and armatures don't.

You want to be successful in business? Don't be like the original owner of that land who gave up just when he was inches away from becoming mega rich. Instead, be like the second man who knew the value of seeking advice from experts so he doesn't waste more time doing trial by error.

CONCLUSION

There is money on the internet...so much money. The internet era has produced much more millionaires than any era in the past...and the way I see it; this is just the beginning. And the good news is, the internet is not choosy.

Anybody can make themselves rich, if only they can avoid these pitfalls I highlighted in this book you just read.

You already have an unfair advantage over the many people hustling to make it online and struggling each day without knowing exactly what is keeping them running round a circle. Now it's left for you to decide what you do with this information.

I hope you join the top 5 percent of the people who are making 95 percent of the money online. I believe you can do it. The question is: Do you believe you can do it? Do you believe you can become rich building businesses online?

MEET KINGSLEY OKORO

I am one person who has always been in love with the idea of working from home and making money from the comfort of my bedroom.

After losing my first (traditional) business back in 2009, I was broke, hopeless, frustrated and didn't know what else to do with my life. My experience with internet business started the day I saw an ad on a newspaper with the caption, "Income Opportunity With Google". Before then, I never knew there was a way to make money online.

I bundled up the last N10,000 I had and went to the bank to pay for this guide. I didn't even have a laptop or a smartphone, so when the material I paid for was sent to my Email, I had to go to a cyber café to download and print it out. It was a bundle containing 3 eBooks.

I spent the next couple of weeks studying those materials without really understanding what I was expected to do next. Just a bunch of internet jargons I'd never really heard before, like SEO, Adsense, Domain name, Hosting, SSL, etc.

Buying those eBooks didn't make me money, but it opened my eyes to a reality I never had before. I came to realize that it was actually possible to make money from the comfort of my home, leveraging the internet to provide some sort of value that people would be willing to pay for.

So far, I have used the internet to do business and make money in different industries: Network marketing, affiliate marketing, selling of physical products, and even creating and selling digital products.

And I know that what gave me the freedom I enjoy today—the freedom to never have to look for job ever again—is the digital marketing skills I have gathered over the years.

With the skills I now have, I have also been able to impact the lives of others through my training and mentorship.

I started The Kings Organization for the purpose of reaching out to more people who are still trapped in the unemployment—or underemployment—cycle.

My goal is to help people create the lifestyle of their dream by leveraging the same power of financial education and digital marketing skills that gave me my own freedom.

Through The Kings Organization, we will empower thousands of individuals to become masters of money rather than being slaves to it.

Ready With Your Manuscript?

"BECOME A PUBLISHED AUTHOR OF A BESTSELLING EBOOK WITHOUT THE USUAL HUSTLE!"

We will turn your manuscript into a highly sort after eBook that turns in consistent cash flow for you, using our professional editing, designing and publishing service.

Chat with Us Now

www.ingramcontent.com/pod-product-compliance
Lightning Source LLC
Chambersburg PA
CBHW062249290526
45794CB00006B/2471